JAPANESE EQUIPMENT

PHOTOGRAPHS AND CHARACTERISTICS OF
BASIC WEAPONS ENCOUNTERED IN SWPA

The Naval & Military Press Ltd

Published by

The Naval & Military Press Ltd
Unit 5 Riverside, Brambleside
Bellbrook Industrial Estate
Uckfield, East Sussex
TN22 1QQ England

Tel: +44 (0)1825 749494

www.naval-military-press.com
www.nmarchive.com

FOREWORD

Gratitude is expressed to those Officers and Men who have forwarded specimens of captured equipment to Intelligence. Their co-operation has greatly assisted in the production of this Booklet.

Carry it with you always, for it will provide a ready reference to Japanese weapons most frequently encountered in the SWPA.

Only tanks reported as being used by the Japanese in this or adjacent areas have been mentioned. Badges of rank have been included for general information.

Much has still to be done before we fully know the Jap. To achieve this, Intelligence largely depends on troops in contact with the enemy. No detail is too small to report. Your help is vital.

TABLE OF CONTENTS.

TABLE OF CONTENTS—continued.

iv.

DISTINGUISHING FLAGS AND BADGES

ARMY INSIGNIA

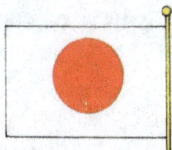

NATIONAL FLAG
Carried by sections
to indicate position

NAVAL ENSIGN
Carried by Special
Naval Landing Parties

NAVAL INSIGNIA

BATTALION FLAGS

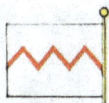

1 BN.

2 BN.

3 BN.

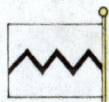

1 RESERVE BN.

2 RESERVE BN.

3 RESERVE BN.

One

BADGES OF RANK—NCOs

WORN:—TUNIC: On shoulder or collar—SHIRT: On either pocket

SERJEANT MAJOR

SERJEANT

CORPORAL

SUPERIOR PRIVATE

1st CLASS PRIVATE

2nd CLASS PRIVATE

BADGES WORN ON RIGHT ARM ABOVE ELBOW

N C O

ACTING CORPORAL

SUPERIOR PRIVATE

ACTING SUP PTE

Two

BADGES OF RANK—OFFICERS

WORN:—TUNIC: On shoulder or collar—SHIRT: On either pocket

GENERAL

LIEUT-GENERAL

MAJOR-GENERAL

COLONEL

LIEUT-COLONEL

MAJOR

CAPTAIN

LIEUTENANT

2nd LIEUTENANT

WARRANT OFFICER

Three

8 mm AUTOMATIC PISTOL Model "14" ("NAMBU")

SAFETY CATCH
OFF   ON

COCKING
KNOB

PLATFORM
STUD
(Depress to
allow rapid
filling of
magazine)

LANYARD LOOP

MAGAZINE
CATCH

MAGAZINE
CAPACITY
8 ROUNDS

STOCK RETAINING SCREW
(Remove on commencement
of stripping)

Four

8 mm AUTOMATIC PISTOL Model " 14 " (" NAMBU ")

An accurate, high velocity, service automatic. While resembling the 7.65 mm LUGER in size, appearance and balance, it has a mechanism which is entirely different from that of any other pistol.

This pattern has been manufactured in Japan for many years, and normally, is far superior in finish to those being produced under present wartime conditions. Previously this pistol was fitted with an adjustable rear sight and could be fired from the shoulder by means of a special butt attachment.

CHARACTERISTICS.

Calibre — — —	8 mm (.315 in).
Weight — — —	2 lb (approx).
Length, overall — —	9 in.
Length of barrel —	4½ in (including chamber).
Sights — — —	Fixed (open).
Magazine capacity —	8 rounds.
Ammunition — —	Rimless.

OTHER TYPES: Model " 26," " SMITH and WESSON " pattern revolver. Calibre 9 mm; weight 2 lb (approx); capacity 6 rounds.

SCALE OF ISSUE: Most Officers and NCOs.

C

6.5 mm INFANTRY RIFLE "MEIJI 38" (1905)

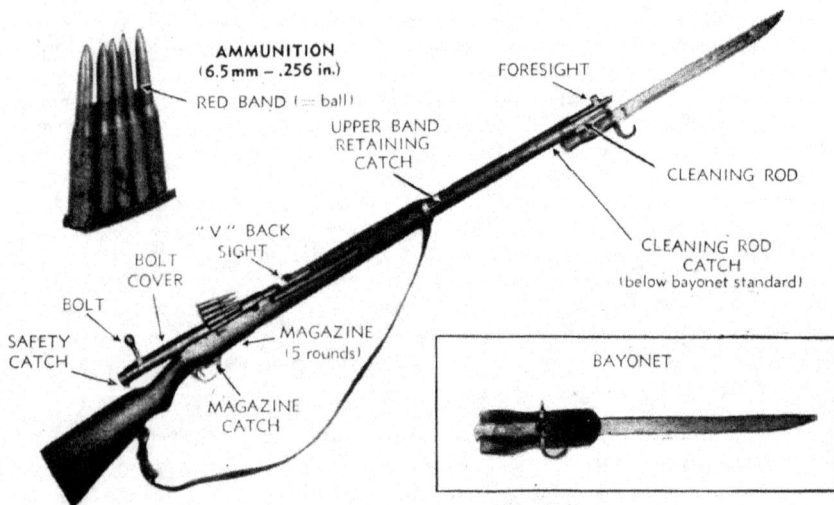

AMMUNITION
(6.5 mm – .256 in.)

RED BAND (= ball)

FORESIGHT

UPPER BAND
RETAINING
CATCH

CLEANING ROD

CLEANING ROD
CATCH
(below bayonet standard)

"V" BACK
SIGHT

BOLT
COVER

BOLT

MAGAZINE
(5 rounds)

SAFETY
CATCH

MAGAZINE
CATCH

BAYONET

6.5 mm INFANTRY RIFLE " MEIJI 38 " (1905)

This is the standard infantry rifle. Although several other types are in use, the " MEIJI 38 " has been the most frequently encountered to date.

While an extreme range of 4,300 yds is claimed, indications are that it is only fairly accurate over 500 yds.

It is considered that eventually it will be supplanted by the 7.7 mm Rifle, Type 99 (see " OTHER TYPES " below).

CHARACTERISTICS.

Calibre — — —	6.5 mm (.256 in).
Length, overall — —	4 ft 2½ in (without bayonet).
Weight — — —	8 lb 12 oz (without bayonet).
Magazine system — —	Fixed, vertical box.
Magazine capacity —	5 rounds.
Bolt action — —	" MAUSER " type, fitted with removable dust cover.
Sight range — —	400—2,400 metres.
Ammunition — —	Rimless, nitro-cellulose charged.

BAYONET: Sword type; length overall 20 in; weight 13 oz. No " boss " is provided, bayonet ring fits over end of barrel.

OTHER TYPES: Model " 99 " closely resembles the " MEIJI 38 " in general design. Calibre 7.7 mm (.303 in); weight 8½ lb; length 3 ft 8 in; capacity 5 rounds. Ammunition is NOT inter-changeable with our weapons.

HAND GRENADE—H E

SAFETY
PIN

FUZE
COVER

FILLER
PLUG
(painted red)

BODY
(50 segments)
painted black

TOP VIEW

HEAD OF
STRIKER

Grenade is SAFE when Head of Striker is
flush with TOP of Fuze Cover

TO ARM GRENADE
With Safety Pin IN, Screw down Striker to full extent

Eight

HAND GRENADE—H E

There are two variations of this grenade, i.e., Types "91" and "97." Grenades are of similar appearance, size and approximate weight. Difference may be ascertained by examination of their base. It is not known definitely to which grenade the respective type numbers apply. Fragmentation from these grenades is poor.

SOLID BASE TYPE: Designed solely for use as a hand grenade. Fuze delay is approximately 4 seconds.

RECESSED BASE TYPE: May be thrown by hand, or fired, by means of an attachment screwed into base, from the rifle (see page 10) or from the Type "89" Grenade Discharger (see page 12). Fuze delay is approximately 7 or 8 seconds.

GENERAL CHARACTERISTICS: Length, 4 in (including fuze); Diameter, 49.7 mm (1.94 in); Weight, 1 lb (approx).

TO THROW: Make sure grenade is armed (see page 8). Grasp grenade with fuze pointing downward. Withdraw safety pin. Strike head of fuze cover sharply against heel of boot or hard object, driving striker into percussion cap. Throw grenade.

WARNING: OWING TO ERRATIC BEHAVIOUR OF FUZES CARE MUST BE TAKEN TO THROW GRENADE **IMMEDIATELY** HEAD OF GRENADE HAS BEEN STRUCK.

RIFLE GRENADES AND POUCH

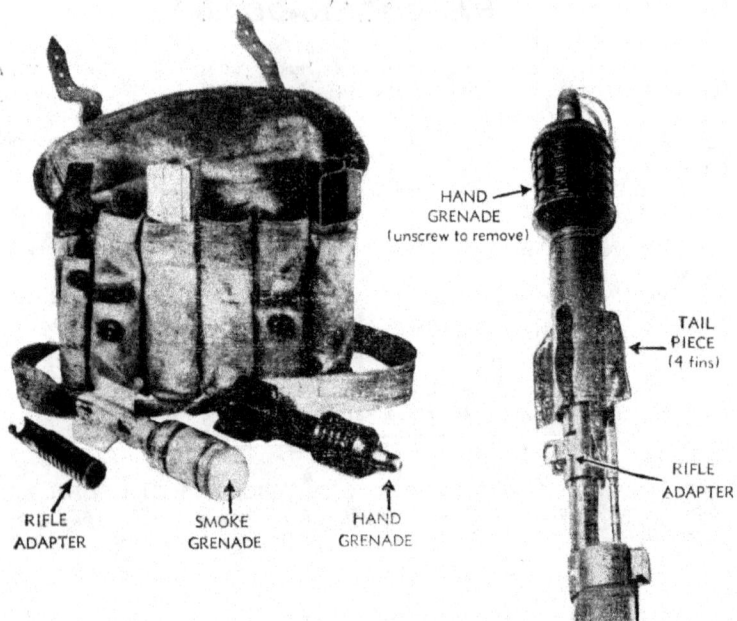

HAND
GRENADE
(unscrew to remove)

TAIL
PIECE
(4 fins)

RIFLE
ADAPTER

RIFLE
ADAPTER

SMOKE
GRENADE

HAND
GRENADE

Ten

RIFLE GRENADES AND POUCH

When firing from the rifle, a finned tail piece is screwed into the base of the grenade. Housed in each tail piece is a specially prepared cartridge. This cartridge is Ballastite filled and fitted with a wooden bullet shaped plug of 6.5 mm (.256 in) calibre. This plug is not removed when cartridge is loaded into the breach.

PREPARATION FOR FIRING.

Place adapter over muzzle of rifle. Rotate in clockwise direction approximately quarter turn, causing foresight block to engage in adapter locking recess.

Remove cartridge from grenade tail piece and load into breech. Place grenade over adapter. Fire rifle in normal manner for discharging grenades.

H E GRENADE.

Before firing, make sure grenade is armed and safety pin removed. Shock of explosion on base of grenade will drive striker into percussion cap.

SMOKE GRENADE (Non Toxic).

Weight 1.29 lb.

There is no fuze to this grenade, action is started by the flash of exploded cartridge.

GRENADE DISCHARGER Type "89" (1929)

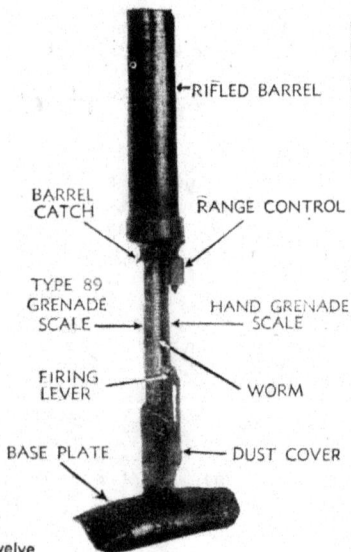

RIFLED BARREL

BARREL CATCH

RANGE CONTROL

TYPE 89 GRENADE SCALE

HAND GRENADE SCALE

FIRING LEVER

WORM

BASE PLATE

DUST COVER

HAND GRENADE
7 SECOND TIME FUZE
MAXIMUM RANGE—
190 METRES
210 YARDS (APPROX.)

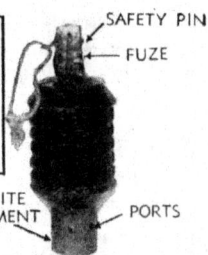

SAFETY PIN

FUZE

BALLASTITE ATTACHMENT

PORTS

SAFETY PIN

TYPE 88 FUZE

TYPE 89 GRENADE
INSTANTANEOUS PERCUSSION FUZE
MAXIMUM RANGE
650 METRES
710 YARDS (APPROX.)

DRIVING BAND

Twelve

GRENADE DISCHARGER Type "89" (1929)

One of the weapons most freely used by the Japanese for Close Support purposes. Also employed during Landing Operations, being fired from the gunwale of Landing Craft. This weapon can NOT be fired from the thigh.

CHARACTERISTICS.

Calibre	— —	50 mm (1.97 in).
Weight	— —	10 lb 1 oz.
Length, overall	—	23.8 in.
Rifling	— —	8 grooves R H.
Range	— —	Type " 89 " Grenade: 120-650 metres (130-710 yds approx).
Range	— —	Hand Grenade: 40-190 metres 44-210 yds approx).

RANGE CONTROL: The worm protruding into the barrel provides a moveable stop for the bomb. Rotation of range control knob, by raising or lowering the worm varies the chamber capacity, thereby altering range.

TO FIRE: With base plate on ground, discharger is held by the LEFT hand at an angle of 45°. Sighting by a vertical RED line on the barrel, distance is judged and range set accordingly. Grenade is dropped down barrel (safety pin removed) and fired by pulling lanyard.

TYPE " 89 " GRENADE: Weight 23 oz TNT filled. When fired, ballastite propelling charge at rear, causes copper driving band to expand and engage in rifling.

OTHER GRENADES: A ballastite attachment may be screwed into base of H E HAND GRENADE. Smoke and flare grenades are also fired.

Thirteen

7.63 mm SMG "SOLOTHURN"

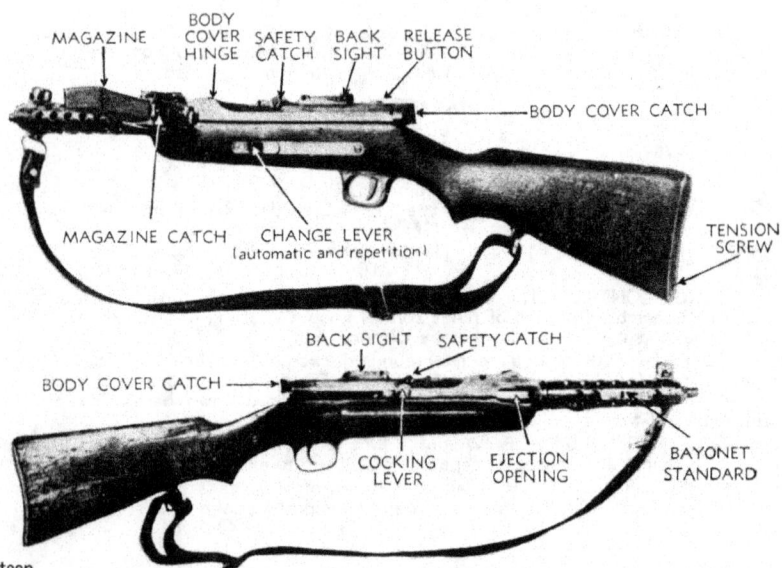

MAGAZINE   BODY COVER HINGE   SAFETY CATCH   BACK SIGHT   RELEASE BUTTON

BODY COVER CATCH

MAGAZINE CATCH   CHANGE LEVER (automatic and repetition)

TENSION SCREW

BACK SIGHT   SAFETY CATCH

BODY COVER CATCH

COCKING LEVER   EJECTION OPENING   BAYONET STANDARD

Fourteen

7.63 mm SMG "SOLOTHURN"

To date the only SMG, captured from the Japanese in this Area. Weapon is of German manufacture and was made under the terms of the Versailles Treaty, which prevented Germany from manufacturing weapons of 9 mm military calibre. To surmount this restriction, weapon was so designed that the 7.63 mm barrel could be removed and a 9 mm barrel substituted. No other change is necessary to complete the conversion. A standard infantry bayonet may be fitted.

CHARACTERISTICS.

Automatic action is brought about by projection of spent case and return spring. Bolt is not locked and works on the blow back principle.

Calibre	—	—	7.63 mm (.300 in).
Length	—	—	32¼ in.
Magazine	—	—	Box type 30/32 rounds.
Rate of fire	—	—	700 rpm.
Type of fire	—	—	Single/automatic.
Type of sights	—	—	Open.
Sight range	—	—	0-500 metres.

CHANGE LEVER: Operation is similar to that of the " Bren " LMG.

6.5 mm LMG TAISHO II (1922) "NAMBU"

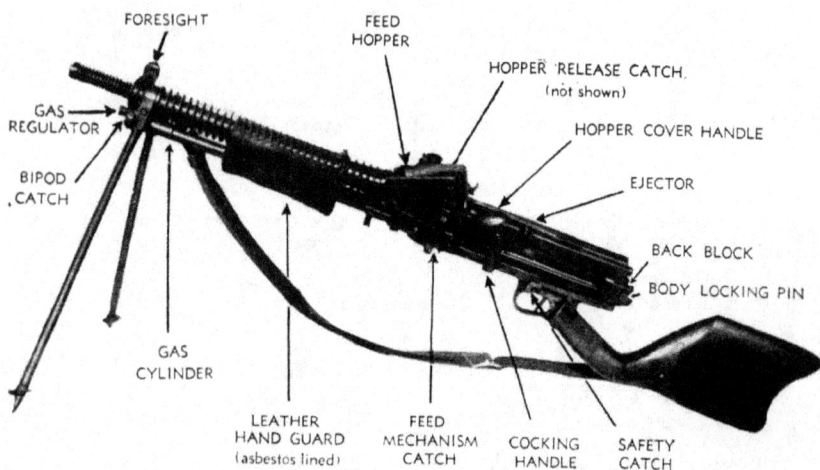

FORESIGHT

FEED HOPPER

HOPPER RELEASE CATCH. (not shown)

HOPPER COVER HANDLE

GAS REGULATOR

EJECTOR

BIPOD CATCH

BACK BLOCK

BODY LOCKING PIN

GAS CYLINDER

LEATHER HAND GUARD (asbestos lined)

FEED MECHANISM CATCH

COCKING HANDLE

SAFETY CATCH

6.5 mm LMG TAISHO II (1922) " NAMBU "

Although being replaced gradually by the later model LMG, Type " 96 " (see pages 18/19), the TAISHO II is still frequently encountered. Weapon may be identified by its unusually shaped butt.

CHARACTERISTICS.

Gun is gas operated, air cooled, and bipod mounted. Method of feed, consisting of a hopper attached to the LEFT side of the body, is unique. A bad feature is the unprotected " Lewis " type ejector, which is liable to damage.

Calibre — — —	6.5 mm (.256 in).
Weight of gun — —	22 lb 7 oz.
Length, overall — —	43½ in.
Hopper capacity —	30 rounds (6 clips of 5 rounds).
Maximum rate of fire —	500 rpm.
Practical rate of fire —	120 rpm (approx).
Type of fire — —	Automatic only.
Sights — — —	Backsight graduated from 300-1,500 metres.
Ammunition — —	As fired from rifle.

PREPARATION FOR FIRING: Raise cover of feed hopper and insert six clips of cartridges. Bring down hopper cover, so that it bears against the uppermost clip. Pull back cocking handle until bent of piston engages with sear. Gun is now cocked. Carry cocking handle fully forward. Gun is now ready for firing.

6.5 mm LMG Type "96" (1936)

GAS REGULATOR

CARRYING HANDLE (fixed)

BARREL LOCKING CATCH

FIXED FOCUS TELESCOPIC SIGHT

LOCKING KNOB

MAGAZINE CATCH

BLOCK FOR TELESCOPIC SIGHT

DRUM SIGHT

BODY LOCKING PIN

BIPOD RELEASE CATCH

BAYONET STANDARD

COCKING HANDLE

EJECTOR COVER (not shown)

SAFETY CATCH

BACK BLOCK

6.5 mm LMG Type " 96 " (1936)

A later and improved type of Japanese LMG. While somewhat resembling the British " Bren," it is in no respect a copy of this weapon. Jap MGs of varying calibres are now being built to this design. This weapon has been reported frequently as a SMG, for, while normally fired from a bipod it is also fired from the hip. A standard infantry bayonet may be fitted for hand to hand fighting.

CHARACTERISTICS.

Calibre — —	6.5 mm (.256 in).
Weight —	21 lb.
Length overall —	42 in.
Magazine — —	" Bren " type. 30 rounds.
Maximum rate of fire	530 rpm. (approx).
Practical rate of fire	120 rpm (approx).
Type of fire — —	Automatic only.
Muzzle velocity —	2410 fps.
Sights — —	Drum controlled aperture rearsight 200-1,600 metres.
Ammunition —	As fired from rifle.

TELESCOPIC SIGHT: A small fixed focus telescopic sight is frequently used with this weapon. Magnification 2 X; field of view 13.4 degrees. Sight is mounted on a block at top right rear of body.

7.7 mm HMG Type "92" (1922) "JUKI"

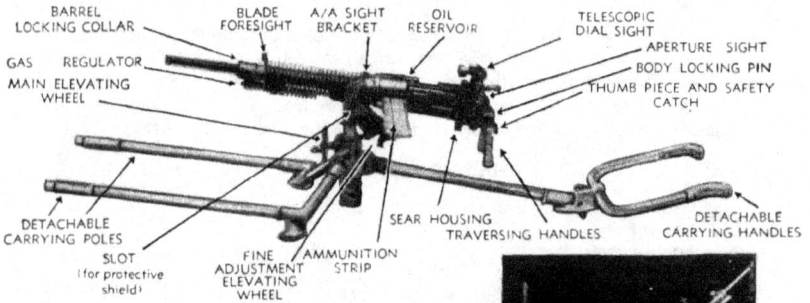

BARREL LOCKING COLLAR
BLADE FORESIGHT
A/A SIGHT BRACKET
OIL RESERVOIR
TELESCOPIC DIAL SIGHT
GAS REGULATOR
MAIN ELEVATING WHEEL
APERTURE SIGHT
BODY LOCKING PIN
THUMB PIECE AND SAFETY CATCH
DETACHABLE CARRYING POLES
SLOT (for protective shield)
FINE ADJUSTMENT ELEVATING WHEEL
AMMUNITION STRIP
SEAR HOUSING
TRAVERSING HANDLES
DETACHABLE CARRYING HANDLES

AMMUNITION STRIP (30 ROUNDS)
COLOUR BANDS :—

RED = ball BLACK = AP GREEN = tracer

block a

7.7 mm HMG Type " 92 " (1922) " JUKI "

While actually a MMG, weapon is classified by the Japanese as HMG
(" JUKI " = heavy). Gun is an improved model of the 1914 Japanese 6.5 mm
(.256 in) " HOTCHKISS " type MG, which it very closely resembles. The latter
weapon is shown in an A/A role on the opposite page. The " JUKI " is similarly
mounted for A/A. For carrying purposes, handles are fitted into brackets on the
tripod legs; this enables the gun, when mounted, to be carried by a team of four
men—two men would suffice over a short distance.

CHARACTERISTICS.

Gun is gas operated, air cooled, strip fed and when in action is identified by
its slow rate of fire—being nicknamed by troops in the New Guinea Area, " The
Woodchopper " or " Woodpecker."

Calibre	— —	7.7 mm (.303 in).
Weight of gun	—	63 lb.
Weight of tripod	—	66½ lb.
Length of gun	—	46 in.
Type of feed	—	Strip (30 rounds).
Maximum rate of fire		400—600 rpm.
Type of fire	—	Automatic only.
Sights	— —	Tangent column, aperture backsight.
Ammunition	—	Rimless—will not fi: British weapons.

DIAL SIGHT: A fixed focus telescopic dial sight is used for indirect fire.
Magnification 4 X; field of view 10 degrees.

13 mm DOUBLE BARREL A/A-TK/A GUN Type "93" (1933)

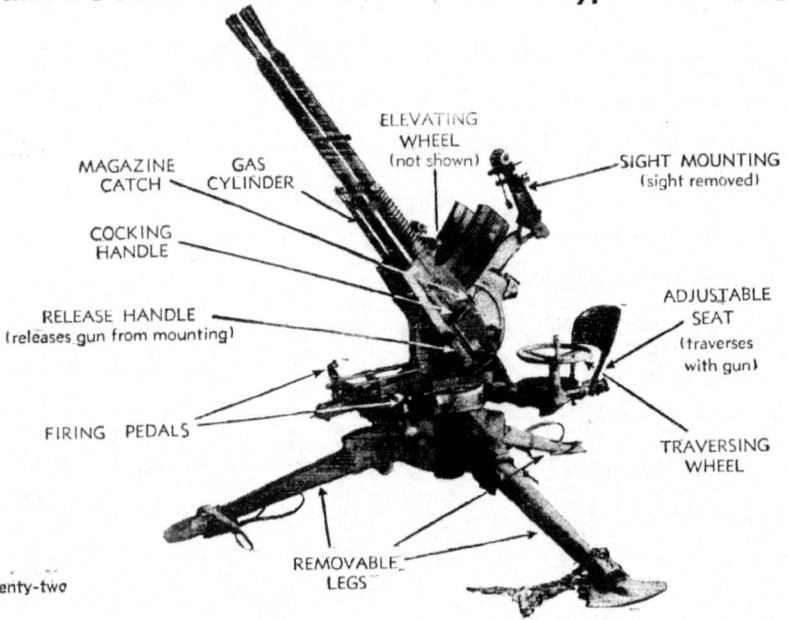

MAGAZINE CATCH

GAS CYLINDER

ELEVATING WHEEL (not shown)

SIGHT MOUNTING (sight removed)

COCKING HANDLE

RELEASE HANDLE (releases gun from mounting)

ADJUSTABLE SEAT (traverses with gun)

FIRING PEDALS

TRAVERSING WHEEL

REMOVABLE LEGS

13 mm DOUBLE BARREL A/A-TK/A GUN Type " 93 " (1933)

In accordance with the Japanese principle of constructing dual purpose weapons, this HMG may be used for both A/A-TK/A purposes.

CHARACTERISTICS.

Mounting is designed to carry two units allowing an elevation of 85° and a traverse of 360°. Guns are separately mounted and may be removed from the cradle by means of independent release handles. Seat, elevating and traversing gear all traverse with gun. Weapon is fired by foot pedals situated at either end of crossbar, to which is fitted foot plates and firing rod controls. The following details apply only to a single unit:—

Calibre — — — —	13.15 mm (.52 in).
Weight of gun — —	87 lb.
Weight of magazine (empty)	5 lb.
Length of barrel — —	65 in.
(including flash eliminator)	
Magazine capacity — —	30 rounds.
Maximum rate of fire —	450-480 rpm.
Type of fire — — —	Automatic.
Sights — — — —	200-3,600 metres.
(leaf backsight not used for A/A)	

TYPES and MARKINGS OF AMMUNITION: WHITE = ball; BLACK = AP; RED = tracer.

SAFETY PRECAUTIONS: As there is no safety catch, care must be taken when weapon is loaded.

20 mm A/A-TK/A GUN Type "98" (1938)

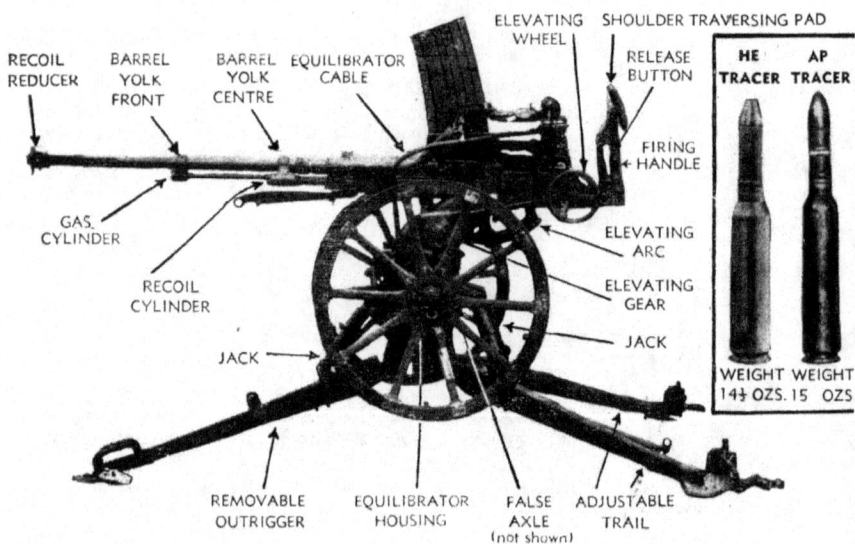

RECOIL REDUCER

BARREL YOLK FRONT

BARREL YOLK CENTRE

EQUILIBRATOR CABLE

ELEVATING WHEEL

SHOULDER TRAVERSING PAD

RELEASE BUTTON

FIRING HANDLE

GAS CYLINDER

RECOIL CYLINDER

ELEVATING ARC

ELEVATING GEAR

JACK

JACK

REMOVABLE OUTRIGGER

EQUILIBRATOR HOUSING

FALSE AXLE (not shown)

ADJUSTABLE TRAIL

HE TRACER

AP TRACER

WEIGHT 14½ OZS.

WEIGHT 15 OZS.

20 mm A/A-TK/A GUN Type "98" (1938)

A dual purpose gun of " Oerlikon " type, which is now being manufactured in Japan.

CHARACTERISTICS.

Mounting is so designed that by opening the trail and attaching an outrigger a tripod is formed. Wheels are then removed, allowing the gun a 360° free traverse. It is not necessary to remove wheels unless the full traverse is required. In an emergency, gun may be fired as a split trail field piece. Weapon is shoulder controlled.

Calibre — —	20 mm (.79 in).
Total weight —	840 lb.
Length of barrel	57¼ in (including recoil reducer).
Magazine —	" Bren " type, 20 rounds.
Elevation —	+ 85°; Depression — 10°.
Rate of fire —	120 rpm.
Type of fire —	Automatic/Repetition.
Maximum range	Horizontal: 5,450 yds; Vertical: 12,000 ft.

TO FIRE: Release button on firing handle must be depressed before handle can be pushed forward, firing gun.

25 mm TRIPLE BARREL A/A-TK/A GUN

INDEPENDENT MAGAZINES

SIGHTING GEAR

ELEVATION WHEEL AND SEAT
(not shown)

ELEVATING ARC

TRAVERSING WHEEL AND SEAT

FLASH ELIMINATORS

25 mm TRIPLE BARREL A/A-TK/A GUN

This dual purpose gun is of Naval origin. It is reported that such weapons are mounted as single, double and triple combinations.

Full information is not available at present, the only specimen captured to date in the SWPA being incomplete.

CHARACTERISTICS.

Weapon consists of three, gas operated, air cooled units each being fed from a separate magazine. Loading principle is very similar to that of the " Bren." The ejection opening is in the bottom of the body.

Range and elevating gear is on the LEFT and traversing gear on the RIGHT. A steel seat, traversing with the gun, is provided on either side for gun layers.

Calibre	—	—	25 mm (.98 in).
Length of barrel	—	—	5 ft 9½ in.
Magazine capacity	—		15 rounds.
Elevation	—	—	—	75°.
Traverse	—	—	—	360°.
Ammunition	—	—	H E and H E-tracer.

37 mm TK/A GUN Type "94" (1934)

AMMUNITION PANNIER
CAPACITY 12 ROUNDS
WEIGHT WHEN FULL 45 LB.

ELEVATING
WHEEL
(gun fired by
pulling to rear)

RANGE
CONTROL
WHEEL

HE SHELL
WEIGHT
26 OZS.

AP BASE
FUZED SHELL
WEIGHT
28 OZS.

TRAVERSING
WHEEL

ADJUSTABLE
SPLIT TRAIL

LEVER BREECH
MECHANISM

TOWING
LUGS

Twenty-eight

37 mm TK/A Gun Type "94" (1934)

Known to the Japanese as "Rapid fire" guns they provide front line infantry with direct close protection from attack by hostile AFVs. Weapon is also used as a light field piece, firing H E ammunition.

CHARACTERISTICS.

Gun has a semi automatic, horizontal sliding breech block.

Firing gear is connected to the elevating hand wheel, which, when pulled to the rear fires gun. Recoil and recuperation are controlled by oil buffer and helical spring.

Carriage is of split trail type, normally mounted on iron wheels. Others are mounted on iron shod wooden wheels.

Calibre	−	−	−	37 mm (1.4 in).
Total weight	−	−	−	815 lb.
Length of bore	−	−	−	4 ft 10 in.
Length of trail	−	−	−	5 ft 5½ in.
Traverse	−	−	−	60°.
Elevation	−	−	−	+ 25°; Depression − 8°.
Muzzle velocity	−	−	−	2,300 fps.
Maximum range	−	−	−	5,500 yds.
Rate of fire	−	−	−	25 rpm.

Gun is accurate and easy to fire but examination of ammunition shows that penetration would be comparatively poor.

OTHER TYPES: 47 mm TK/A guns, mounted on rubber tyred wheels have been reported in adjoining areas.

70 mm BATTALION GUN Type "92" (1932)

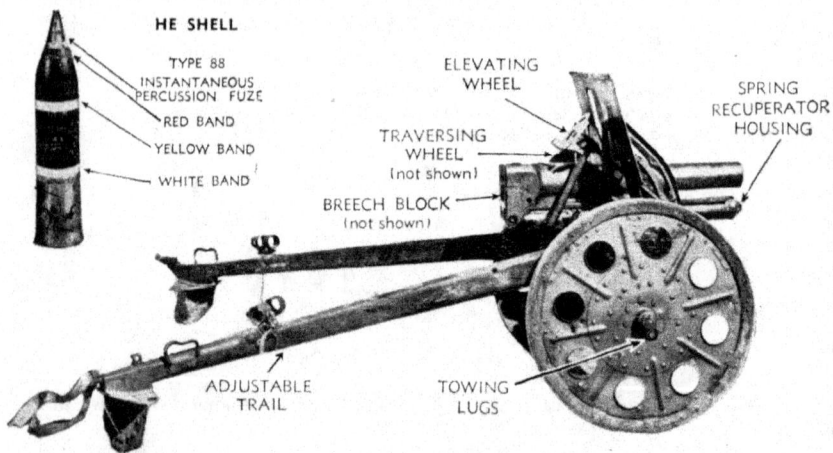

HE SHELL

TYPE 88
INSTANTANEOUS
PERCUSSION FUZE
RED BAND
YELLOW BAND
WHITE BAND

ELEVATING
WHEEL

SPRING
RECUPERATOR
HOUSING

TRAVERSING
WHEEL
(not shown)

BREECH BLOCK
(not shown)

ADJUSTABLE
TRAIL

TOWING
LUGS

Thirty

70 mm BATTALION GUN Type "92" (1932)

A close support weapon issued on a scale of two guns per Infantry Battalion. It is stated to be not very efficient and viewed somewhat unfavourably by the Japanese.

CHARACTERISTICS.

This weapon is a miniature howitzer characterized by a low muzzle velocity. It is employed in the tactical role of a long range mortar.

Ammunition is semi-fixed and range is controlled by varying the powder charge.

Calibre — — —	70 mm (2.75 in).
Weight — — —	470 lb (approx).
Length of Barrel — —	28½ in.
Length of Bore — —	24¼ in.
Traverse — — —	40°.
Elevation — — —	+ 50°; Depression — 10°.
Maximum Range — —	3,000 yds.
Muzzle Velocity — —	650 fps.

HE. projectile weighs 8 pounds and is fitted with a Type "88" percussion fuze. It is interesting to note that this fuze is also used with shells of 75 mm and 105 mm calibres.

75 mm REGIMENTAL GUN Type "41" (1908)

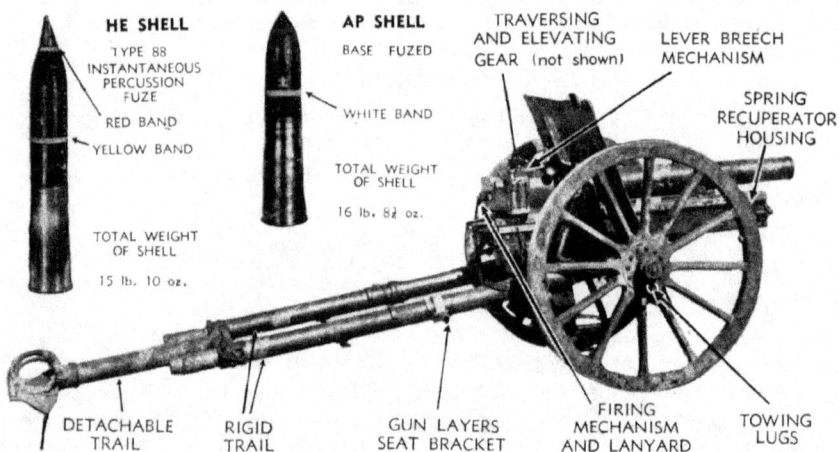

HE SHELL

TYPE 88
INSTANTANEOUS
PERCUSSION
FUZE

RED BAND

YELLOW BAND

TOTAL WEIGHT
OF SHELL

15 lb. 10 oz.

AP SHELL

BASE FUZED

WHITE BAND

TOTAL WEIGHT
OF SHELL

16 lb. 8½ oz.

TRAVERSING
AND ELEVATING
GEAR (not shown)

LEVER BREECH
MECHANISM

SPRING
RECUPERATOR
HOUSING

DETACHABLE
TRAIL

RIGID
TRAIL

GUN LAYERS
SEAT BRACKET

FIRING
MECHANISM
AND LANYARD

TOWING
LUGS

75 mm REGIMENTAL GUN Type " 41 " (1908)

Prior to 1935 this was the standard weapon of the Mountain Artillery Units. Under a rearmament scheme commenced at this date, provision was made for equipping such Units with a new Model Mountain Gun, the Type " 94 " (see page 48).

Old guns thus liberated were given, on a scale of 4 guns, to each Infantry regiment and placed under the command of the Regimental Commander.

Apparently this plan has not been fully completed as certain artillery units are still equipped with the Type " 41."

CHARACTERISTICS.

Calibre — — — —	75 mm (2.95 in).
Weight — — —	1,220 lb.
Length of barrel — —	4 ft 6½ in.
Length of bore — —	3 ft 7½ in.
Traverse — — —	7°.
Elevation — — —	+ 25°; Depression — 8°.
Breech — — — —	Interrupted screw type.
Maximum range — —	7,000 yds.
Muzzle velocity — —	1,250 fps.

Gun is mounted on two iron shod, wooden wheels, and is readily identified by a rigid tubular box trail.

75 mm MOBILE A/A GUN Type "88" (1928)

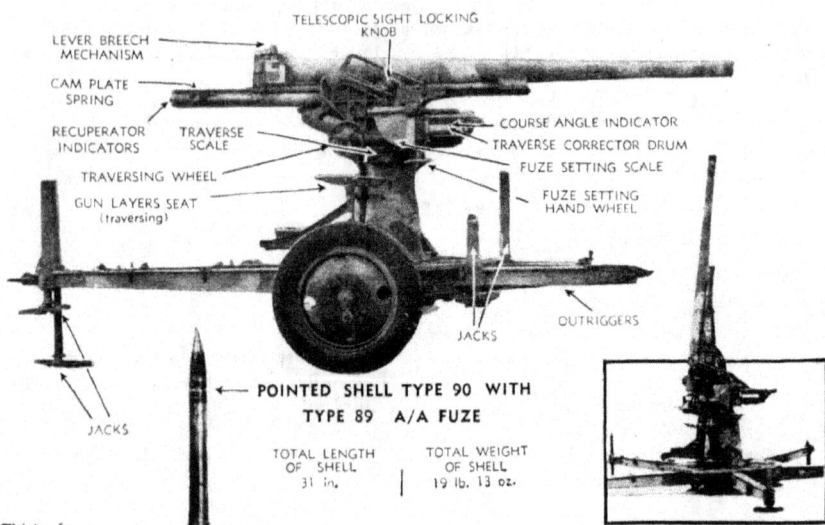

LEVER BREECH MECHANISM

TELESCOPIC SIGHT LOCKING KNOB

CAM PLATE SPRING

RECUPERATOR INDICATORS

TRAVERSE SCALE

COURSE ANGLE INDICATOR

TRAVERSE CORRECTOR DRUM

FUZE SETTING SCALE

TRAVERSING WHEEL

GUN LAYERS SEAT (traversing)

FUZE SETTING HAND WHEEL

JACKS

OUTRIGGERS

JACKS

POINTED SHELL TYPE 90 WITH
TYPE 89 A/A FUZE

TOTAL LENGTH
OF SHELL
31 in.

TOTAL WEIGHT
OF SHELL
19 lb. 13 oz.

Thirty-four

75 mm MOBILE A/A GUN Type "88" (1928)

An improved model of the Japanese M1922 pattern A/A Gun and is believed to be the standard 75 mm weapon in use at present by the Japanese Army. Gun is mobile being mounted on two rubber wheels. When towed, trail and outrigger are brought together and barrel run back on full recoil. In a fixed position wheels are removed, and trail and outriggers opened. An additional outrigger is then attached —all legs are equidistant making a five point base. Levelling of this base is carried out by jacks situated at end of trail and outriggers.

CHARACTERISTICS.

Calibre — — —	75 mm (2.95 in).
Total Weight — —	5,300 lb (approx).
Length of Barrel — —	10 ft 10½ in.
Elevation — — —	0° to 85°.
Traverse — — —	360°.
Horizontal Range — —	15,100 yds.
Vertical Range — —	29,500 ft.
Muzzle Velocity — —	2,360 fps.
Maximum Fuze Setting —	30 seconds.

This gun is a dual purpose weapon and has been employed against AFVs. When used in this manner time fuze is set on safe.

MAGNETIZED AP BOMB Type "99" (1939)

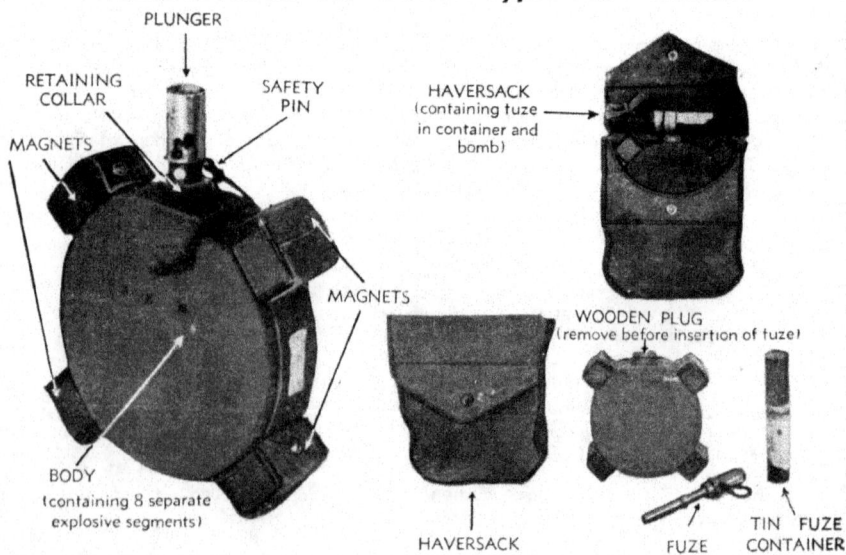

PLUNGER

RETAINING COLLAR

SAFETY PIN

MAGNETS

HAVERSACK
(containing fuze in container and bomb)

MAGNETS

WOODEN PLUG
(remove before insertion of fuze)

BODY
(containing 8 separate explosive segments)

HAVERSACK

FUZE

TIN FUZE CONTAINER

MAGNETIZED A P BOMB Type "99" (1939)

These bombs are intended for use against AFVs and doors of pill-boxes etc. While probably designed to be thrown by hand, loss of magnetic power due to rust and time etc, may necessitate the bomb being brought by hand to the objective— the attacker endeavouring to make his escape during the period of fuze delay.

CHARACTERISTICS.

Bomb consists of eight separate sections of highly compressed explosive contained in khaki cloth covering.

Diameter	— —	$4\frac{3}{4}$ in.
Thickness	— —	$1\frac{1}{2}$ in.
Weight with fuze	—	2 lb 11 oz.

When bomb is carried in haversack fuze hole is filled by a wooden plug $3\frac{3}{4}$ in long. This is removed to permit fitting of fuze. Fuze is secured in bomb by screwing down brass locking collar.

ACTION.

To fire bomb withdraw safety pin and depress aluminium plunger.

WARNING: ALTHOUGH A RECENTLY EXAMINED SPECIMEN HAD A FUZE DELAY OF 10 SECONDS, IT IS STRESSED THAT CARE MUST BE OBSERVED OWING TO ERRATIC BEHAVIOUR OF JAPANESE FUZES.

LAND MINE Type "93" (1933)

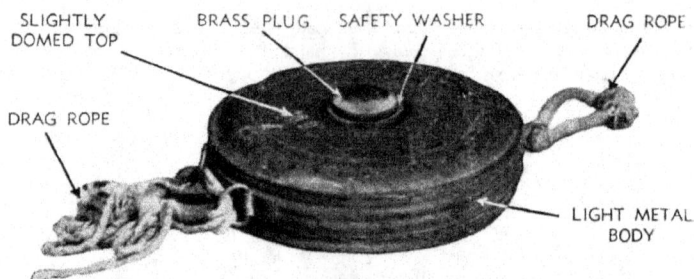

SLIGHTLY DOMED TOP

BRASS PLUG   SAFETY WASHER

DRAG ROPE

DRAG ROPE

LIGHT METAL BODY

BRASS PLUG

FUZE

PLUNGER   SAFETY CAP (screws into plunger)

SHEAR WIRE

THREADED BASE

SAFETY WASHER

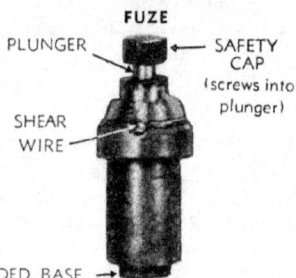

SAFETY COLLAR

Thirty-eight

LAND MINE Type "93" (1933)

Body is in two sections and painted a dull BROWN. A ¾ in RED band is painted around the brass plug which screws into the centre of the body and covers the fuze.

CHARACTERISTICS.

Weight	–	–	3 lb.
Thickness	–	–	1¾ in.
Diameter	–	–	6¾ in.
Filling	–	–	2 lb Picric Compound.

SAFETY DEVICES.

A small safety cap screws into upper end of plunger (striker). When in position, this prevents plunger being depressed and mine exploded. An additional safety device is provided by a brass collar attached to the safety washer. Collar passes over brass safety cap, and surrounding washer is retained beneath brass plug.

SHEARWIRE: This retains the striker when the safety cap and safety collar are removed and alone determines the pressure necessary to fire the mine. The thickness of the wire may vary with the tactical situation.

TO NEUTRALIZE MINE.

(a) Examine area around mine for traps.
(b) Without moving mine or exerting any pressure on cover, unscrew and remove brass plug.
(c) Without downward pressure screw safety cap tightly into top of plunger. Place safety collar over safety cap. Screw on brass plug.

TO DISARM MINE.

(a) Without exerting any downward pressure unscrew brass plug.
(b) Unscrew and remove whole fuze assembly from base of mine.

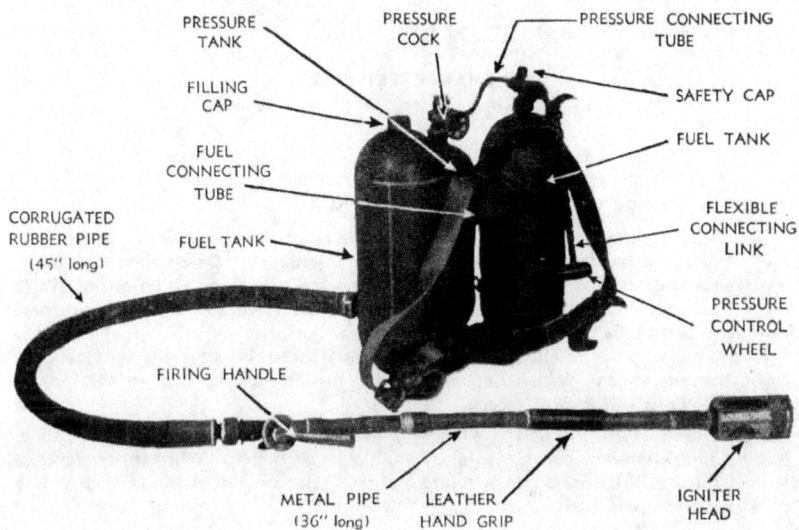

FLAME THROWER Model "93" (1933)

PRESSURE TANK

PRESSURE COCK

PRESSURE CONNECTING TUBE

FILLING CAP

SAFETY CAP

FUEL CONNECTING TUBE

FUEL TANK

CORRUGATED RUBBER PIPE (45" long)

FUEL TANK

FLEXIBLE CONNECTING LINK

PRESSURE CONTROL WHEEL

FIRING HANDLE

METAL PIPE (36" long)

LEATHER HAND GRIP

IGNITER HEAD

FLAME THROWER Model "93" (1933)

This equipment is carried and operated by one man, no special protective clothing being worn.

CHARACTERISTICS.

Weight when charged   –   55 lb (approx).
Fuel capacity –   –   – $2\frac{1}{2}$ gallons (approx).
Type of fuel –   –   –   50% Benzine/Crude Oil.
Duration of flame   –   –   10/12 sec.
Range of flame   –   –   60/80 ft.

ACTION: Pressure cock on head of pressure cylinder is used when pressure tank is disconnected from rest of equipment for re-charging. On charged tank being replaced and connected, cock is opened, allowing pressure to be taken against valve controlled by flexible connecting link. Opening this valve allows pressure to pass into fuel tanks. By rotating firing handle in a clockwise direction, fuel is forced through metal pipe. Simultaneously the igniter head is actuated, automatically firing the fuel stream. When not in use firing handle must be kept in the forward position, otherwise fuel will escape.

IGNITER HEAD: Action is similar to that of an ordinary revolver. Magazine, housed under knurled collar, contains ten blank cartridges. When firing lever is turned through 90°, magazine is rotated, striker released and cartridge fired. Flash of explosion ignites fuel stream.

JAPANESE TANKETTE
TYPE: M 2592 (1932)

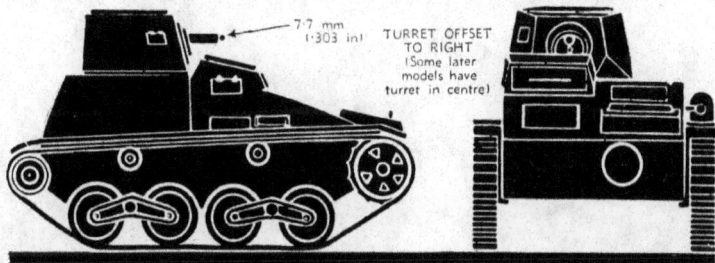

7·7 mm (·303 in) TURRET OFFSET TO RIGHT (Some later models have turret in centre)

CHARACTERISTICS		POINTS TO NOTE
WEIGHT ..	3 tons	I ONE 7·7 mm **MG**, IN FRONT TURRET.
LENGTH ..	10 ft 2 ins	II ROUNDED TURRET, WITH FLAT FRONT, MOUNTED REAR OF HULL STRUCTURE GIVING "BOOT SHAPED" IMPRESSION.
WIDTH ..	5 ft 9 ins	
HEIGHT ..	5 ft 4 ins	III LONG SLOPING FRONT.
SUSPENSION ..	CARDEN-LLOYD TYPE	IV ENGINE IN **LEFT** FRONT.
ARMOUR ..	FRONT/TURRET 14 mm (·55") SIDES 8 mm (·31")	V EXHAUST IN **LEFT** REAR CORNER.
		VI FOUR BOGIE WHEELS IN TWO PAIRS.
CREW ..	2	VII BOGIE BRACKET IS APEX UPWARDS.
SPEED ..	30 mph (ON ROAD)	VIII TWO SUPPORT ROLLERS.

VULNERABLE TO ·55 RIFLE AND 2 PDR **TK/A** GUN.
THIS TYPE WAS FREQUENTLY USED DURING **CHINA** CAMPAIGN AND RECENTLY REPORTED TO HAVE BEEN LANDED AT **LAE**.

Forty-three

JAPANESE LIGHT TANK

MALAYAN TYPE: Possibly M 2595 (1935) Improved

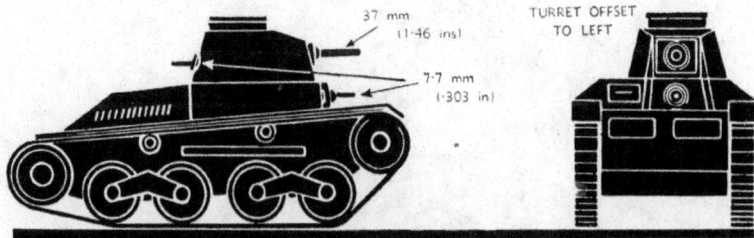

37 mm
(1·46 ins)

7·7 mm
(·303 in)

TURRET OFFSET
TO LEFT

CHARACTERISTICS

WEIGHT	..	9 tons (approx)
LENGTH	..	14 ft 4½ ins
WIDTH	..	6 ft 9 ins
HEIGHT	..	7 ft 0½ ins
SUSPENSION	..	CARDEN-LLOYD TYPE
ARMOUR	..	FRONT/TURRET 12 mm (·47")
		SIDES 10-12 mm (·39-·47")
CREW	..	3-4
SPEED	..	22 mph ON ROAD (REPORTED)

POINTS TO NOTE

I   ONE 37 mm IN TURRET.
II   ONE 7·7 mm **MG** IN REAR OF TURRET.
III ONE 7·7 mm **MG** FRONT OF HULL.
IV   ROUNDED TURRET, POINTED IN REAR, WITH FLAT FRONT.
V   HIGH ENGINE COVER AT REAR.
VI   OVERSIZED EXHAUST AT **RIGHT** REAR.
VII FOUR BOGIE WHEELS IN TWO PAIRS.
VIII BOGIE BRACKET IS APEX UPWARDS.
IX   TWO SUPPORT ROLLERS.

VULNERABLE TO ·55 RIFLE AND 2 PDR **TK/A** GUN.
THIS TYPE WAS FIRST ENCOUNTERED IN **MALAYA**. TWO SIMILAR TANKS WERE
BROUGHT FROM **RABAUL** AND LANDED AT **MILNE BAY**.

JAPANESE MEDIUM TANK
TYPE: M 2594 (1934)

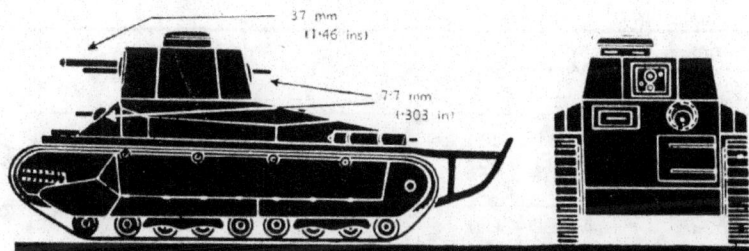

37 mm
(1·46 ins)

7·7 mm
(·303 in)

CHARACTERISTICS		POINTS TO NOTE
WEIGHT	.. 14/16 tons	I ONE 37 mm IN TURRET.
LENGTH	.. 20 ft 10 in (WITH TAIL)	II ONE 7·7 mm **MG** IN REAR OF TURRET.
WIDTH	.. 8 ft 4 ins	III ONE 7·7 mm **MG LEFT** OF FRONT HULL.
HEIGHT	.. 8 ft 6 ins	IV TAIL ON REAR HULL TO INCREASE TRENCH
SUSPENSION	.. COVERED BY ARMOURED SKIRTING	CROSSING PERFORMANCE.
ARMOUR	.. FRONT/TURRET 17 mm (·67")	V STEEP FRONT HULL WITH DOOR ON LEFT.
	.. SIDES 11 mm (·43")	VI IRREGULAR TURRET SET WELL FORWARD.
CREW	.. 5	VII NINE SMALL BOGIE WHEELS ALMOST ENTIRELY
SPEED	.. 28 mph (ON ROAD)	OBSCURED BY SKIRTING.

BELIEVED VULNERABLE TO 2 PDR **TK/A** GUN.
THIS TYPE HAS BEEN USED EXTENSIVELY IN **CHINA** BY BOTH JAPANESE
ARMY AND NAVY. ALSO BELIEVED TO HAVE BEEN USED IN **GUAM**.

Forty-seven

CALIBRE	TYPE	LENGTH OF BORE cals.	M.V. f.s.	WEIGHT OF HE. SHELL lb
75 mm. (2·95 in)	MOUNTAIN GUN. Model " 94 " (1934).	—	1,670	—
75 mm. (2·95 in)	FIELD GUN. " MEIJI 38 " (1905).	30	1,710	14·1 or 13·85
75 mm. (2·95 in)	FIELD GUN. Model " 90 " (1930).	44	2,230	14·3 or 13·85
105 mm. (4·13 in)	HOWITZER. Model " 91 " (1931).	24	1,790	35
105 mm. (4·13 in)	GUN. Model " 92 " (1932).	48	—	33

JAPANESE ARTILLERY

MAXIMUM RANGE yds.	ELEVATION	TRAVERSE	WEIGHT IN ACTION lb	REMARKS
9,800	— 10° to + 40°	39½°	1,200	Replacing the Model " 41 " (1908) REGIMENTAL Gun.
12,600	— 8° to +41° or 43°	7°	2,500	To be replaced by the Model " 90 " (1930).
15,000	— 8° to + 43°	43°	3,000	Future service gun for Divisional Artillery.
14,200	+ 45°	56°	4,250	A new weapon. Believed based on a SCHNEIDER Model. Range also reported as 11,500 yds.
14,200	—	40°	7,700	Range 20,000 yds with streamlined ammunition. A new service model.

CHARACTERISTICS OF JAPANESE MORTARS

TYPE	M.V. fps	RANGE yds	WEIGHT OF BOMB	WEIGHT OF MORTAR	REMARKS
72 mm. (·283 in)	482	— to 1695	4·7 lb	116 lb	This mortar believed to be no longer in use, it s place being taken by the 70 mm. BATTALION Gun. Type " 92."
81 mm. (3·19 in) STOKES BRANDT	656	(i) 545 to 3280 (ii) 207 to 1312	(i) 7·2 lb (ii) 14·3 lb	129·2 lb	(i) Light Bomb. (ii) Heavy Bomb.
90 mm. (3·54 in) MODEL " 94 " (1934)	—	612 to 4155	11·6 lb	350·5 lb	Reported to be used mainly for firing C.W. Bombs.

www.ingramcontent.com/pod-product-compliance
Lightning Source LLC
LaVergne TN
LVHW021130080426
835511LV00010B/1811